Happy Birthday, Baby Jesus

pictures by Ken Munowitz

text by Charles L. Mee, Jr.

Harper & Row, Publishers
New York, Hagerstown, San Francisco, London

For Mom and Irv −K.M.

For Charles − C.M.

HAPPY BIRTHDAY, BABY JESUS

Text copyright © 1976 by Charles L. Mee, Jr.

Illustrations copyright © 1976 by Ken Munowitz

FIRST EDITION

Library of Congress Cataloging in Publication Data

Mee, Charles L., Jr.
    Happy birthday, baby Jesus.

    1. Jesus Christ — Nativity — Juvenile literature.
[1. Jesus Christ — Nativity]   I. Munowitz, Ken.
II. Title.
BT315.2.M37   1976   232.9'2   76-3831
ISBN 0-06-024162-4
ISBN 0-06-024163-2 lib. bdg.

The Bible is a book of stories
thousands of years old.
This is one of the stories of the Bible.

A young girl named Mary and a carpenter named Joseph
discovered that they loved each other.

In heaven,

God told the little angel Gabriel

how happy He was about Mary and Joseph.

"Go to Mary," God told Gabriel,

"and tell her that she will have a baby

and that the baby will be my child."

Gabriel told Mary what God had said.

Later Mary told Joseph what Gabriel had said.

At night,

when Joseph was asleep, he saw Gabriel in a dream,

and the angel said to him,

"Mary's baby is a child of God. And that is good."

Mary and Joseph married and were happy.

They worked, and they thought

about how all children are children of God.

After they had been married for a while,

Mary and Joseph took a trip

to the town of Bethlehem to pay their taxes.

They traveled far

and stopped for the night at an inn.

But there was no room at the inn.

INN

NO
ROOMS

So they slept in the stable with the animals,

And that night,

in the middle of the night,

Jesus was born.

Mary held her baby Jesus,
and Joseph held Mary, and they were pleased.

Outside the stables, in the hills nearby,

an angel went about telling the shepherds

that a child of God had been born.

The shepherds came to the stable to say:
HAPPY BIRTHDAY, BABY JESUS.

In another place, three wise men, called Magi,

looked upon a bright star

and knew a child of God had been born.

The wise men came to the stable
to bring gifts and to say:
HAPPY BIRTHDAY, BABY JESUS.

Everyone was pleased

that a child of God had been born,

and they felt like singing and dancing.

The shepherds were happy,

and the wise men,

and the animals,

and the angels,

and Mary and Joseph,

and they all said:

HAPPY BIRTHDAY, BABY JESUS.

H appy Birthday, Baby Jesus.

J

5
5